Paper Plate MANIA

Christine M. Irvin

Children's Press®
A Division of Scholastic Inc.
New York • Toronto • London • Auckland • Sydney
Mexico City • New Delhi • Hong Kong
Danbury, Connecticut

The author and publisher are not responsible for injuries or accidents that occur during or from any craft projects. Craft projects should be conducted in the presence of or with the help of an adult. Any instructions of the craft projects that require the use of sharp or other unsafe items should be conducted by or with the help of an adult.

Design and Production by Function Thru Form Inc.
Illustrations by Mia Gomez, Function Thru Form Inc
Photographs ©: School Tools/Joe Atlas

Library of Congress Cataloging-in-Publication Data

Irvin, Christine M.
    Paper plate mania / by Christine M. Irvin
        p. cm. — (Craft mania)
    Includes index.
    ISBN 0-516-21675-9 (lib. bdg.)   0-516-27761-8 (pbk.)
    1. Paper work—Juvenile literature. 2. Handicraft—Juvenile literature.
    [1. Paper work. 2. Handicraft.] I. Title. II. Series.

    TT870 .I75 2001
    745.54—dc21

                                              00-046604

Table of Contents

3

Welcome to the World of
CRAFT MANIA!

Don't throw away that paper plate! Everyday items, such as cardboard tubes and paper plates, can become exciting works of art. You can have fun doing the projects and help save the environment at the same time by recycling these household objects instead of just throwing them away.

You can find ways to reuse many things around your home in craft projects. Bottle caps, buttons, old dried beans, and seeds can become eyes, ears, or a nose for an animal. Instead of buying construction paper, you can use scraps of wrapping paper or even last Sunday's comics to cover your art projects. Save the twist ties from bags of bread or vegetables—they make great legs! These are just a few examples of how you can turn garbage into art. Try to think of other things in your home that can be used in your crafts.

Did You Know?

- Each person creates about 4 pounds (1.8 kilograms) of garbage per day.

- Each person in the United States uses about 580 pounds (260 kg) of paper every year. Businesses in the United States use enough paper to circle the earth 20 times every day!

- Americans use enough cardboard each year to make a paper bale as big as a football field.

- Americans throw away more than 60 billion food and drink cans (like tin cans and soft drink cans) and 28 billion glass bottles and jars (like those from ketchup and pickles) every year.

That's a lot of trash!

What you will need

It's easy to get started on your craft projects. The crafts in this book require some materials you can find around your home, some basic art supplies, and your imagination.

Buttons, bottle caps, beads, old dried beans or seeds for decoration

Glue

Tape

Tempera paint

Colored markers

Hole puncher

Construction paper (or newspaper or scraps of wrapping paper)

Felt (or scraps of fabric)

Twist ties (or pipe cleaners)

You might want to keep your craft materials in a box so that they will be ready any time you want to start a craft project. Now that you know what you need, look through the book and pick a project to try. Become a Craft Maniac!

A Note to Grown-Ups

Older children will be able to do most of the projects by themselves. Younger ones will need more adult supervision. All of them will enjoy making the items and playing with their finished creations. The directions for most of the crafts in this book require the use of scissors. Do not allow young children to use scissors without adult supervision.

☞ Helpful Hints

When cutting out shapes from paper plates, it helps to use a ballpoint pen to make a hole first. Hold a pen point down at the center of the shape you want to cut out. With your other hand, carefully pull up on the plate until the pen point pokes through the plate. Now poke your scissors through the hole and cut around the line that you drew.

Halloween Pumpkins

What you need

- **One paper plate** (for each pumpkin)
- **Pencil**
- **Tempera paints, orange and black**
- **Paintbrush**

What you do

1 Paint the paper plate with orange tempera paint. Make sure the paint is completely dry before going on to Step 2.

8

2 Draw a face on your pumpkin plate using the pencil.

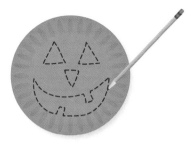

3 Paint over the face that you drew with black paint.

That's it! Your pumpkin is done!

Other Ideas

○ Try making different kinds of faces on your pumpkin, like a scary face or a funny face.

○ Staple two plates together facing each other and decorate both sides.

○ Try adding bits of yarn to your pumpkin's head for hair or a piece of construction paper for a stem.

○ Use your Halloween pumpkin faces as masks.

○ Make a hole at the top using a hole puncher and hang your pumpkin on a string.

○ Use crayons instead of tempera paints to make your pumpkin.

Rhythm Shakers

What you need

- One paper plate for each rhythm shaker
- Dried beans, small beads, or something small and hard
- Masking tape
- Markers or crayons

What you do

1 Fold the paper plate in half.

2 Put some dried beans or other small, dry objects inside the paper plate.

10

3 Tape the edges of the paper plate together, as shown.

4 Decorate your rhythm shaker. Color the paper plate with markers or crayons or paint with tempera paints. Make sure the paint is completely dry before playing with your rhythm shaker.

Now your rhythm shaker is ready to use. Give it a good shake!

Other Ideas

- Experiment with different fillers for your rhythm shakers. Try using rice, tiny pebbles, or buttons.

- Use two paper plates to make a rhythm shaker, instead of folding one paper plate in half.

Creepy Caterpillars

What you need

- **Five paper plates**
  (for each caterpillar)
- **Markers**
- **Hole puncher**
- **Four pieces of ribbon or yarn, each 6 inches long**
- **Pencil**
- **Twist ties**

What you do

1 Make a head for your caterpillar. Using markers, draw a face on one of the plates.

2 Decorate your caterpillar. Using markers, draw stripes or shapes on the other four plates for the body of your caterpillar.

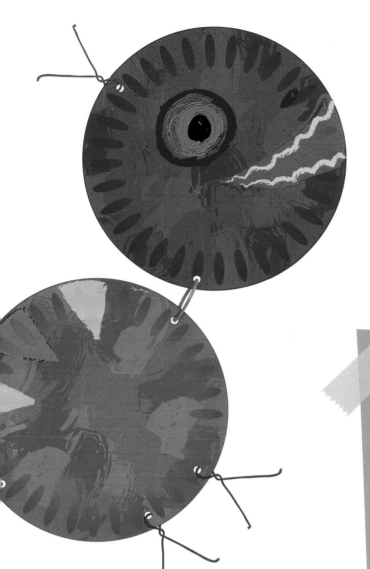

4 Add legs to your caterpillar. Decide how many legs you want on your caterpillar and where you want them. Mark the spots for the legs with a pencil. Use the hole puncher to make the leg holes. Place a twist tie through each hole and wrap the ends together, making two legs.

Other Ideas

- Use smaller paper plates to make a smaller caterpillar, or use a big plate for the head and smaller plates for the body.

- Make a scary sea monster instead of a caterpillar. Draw or paint scales, fins, and a tail.

- Make a caterpillar name plate or banner. Use one paper plate for each letter in your name or your banner message. For instance, you would need four plates for the name Kyle and fourteen plates to say "happy birthday."

3 Put your caterpillar together. Spread your paper plates out on a table with the head on one end and the rest of the plates side-by-side in the order you want them. Using the hole puncher, punch holes in the plates to join the plates together. Tie the plates together with the pieces of ribbon.

Fun With Fish

What you need

- One paper plate
- Pencil
- Scissors (Before cutting any material, please ask an adult for help.)
- Glue
- Tempera paints
- Paintbrush
- Crayons or markers

What you do

1. Cut out the mouth. Turn plate so that the bottom of the plate is facing up. Draw a v-shaped line on the plate where you want the mouth, as shown. Have an adult help you cut out the triangle shape. Save the piece of cut-out plate for the tail, in Step 2.

14

2 Make a tail. Spread a thin layer of glue on the tip of the cut-out tail. Glue it on the back of the plate, across from the mouth, as shown. Let glue dry before going on to Step 3.

3 Decorate your fish. Draw lines on your fish for scales. Paint along the lines with tempera paints. Let paint dry. Color along the lines with crayons or markers. Paint or draw an eye for your fish.

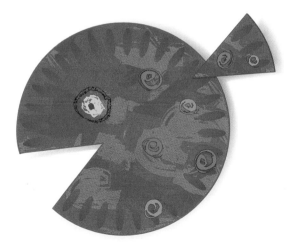

Other Ideas

○ Glue sequins, bits of colored tissue paper, or glitter on your fish for a different look.

○ Color your fish with crayons instead of tempera paints.

○ Make a school of different-sized fish.

Beautiful Butterfly

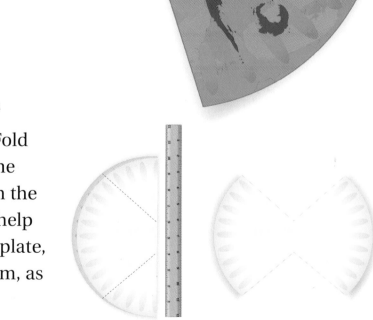

What you need

- **One paper plate**
- **Scissors** (Before cutting any material, please ask an adult for help.)
- **Markers**
- **Long twist ties** (Ones that can be found around vegetables, such as lettuce.)
- **Ruler**

What you do

1 Cut out the butterfly wings. Fold the paper plate in half. Use the ruler to measure a 2-inch section in the middle of the plate. Have an adult help you cut two triangles off the paper plate, one at the top and one at the bottom, as shown. Unfold the paper plate.

16

2 Decorate your butterfly. Use markers to color the butterfly wings.

3 Add the body and antennae. Fold the twist tie in half. Slide the middle of the paper plate butterfly through the twist tie, leaving a small section on one end of the twist tie for the body and about 1 inch at the other end for the antennae. Twist the twist tie ends together at the edge of the paper plate. Spread the antennae open.

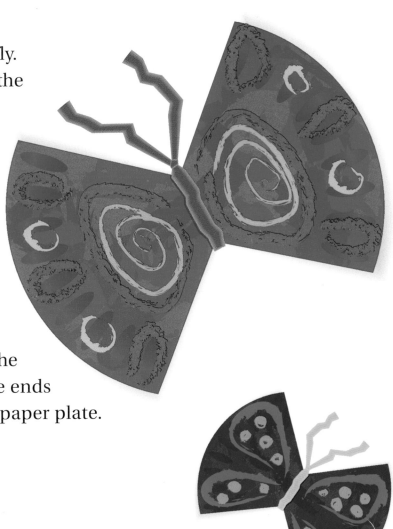

Other Ideas

- Use different-sized plates to make a family of butterflies. Try making each butterfly a different color or a different pattern.

- Try painting your butterfly.

- Use scraps of fabric or wrapping paper to decorate your butterfly.

Seasonal Wreath

What you need

- One paper plate
- Scissors (Before cutting any material, please ask an adult for help.)
- Markers
- Hole puncher
- Small piece of ribbon or yarn
- Pen

What you do

1 Make a wreath shape. Draw a circle in the middle of the plate. Hold a pen point down at the center of the circle you want to cut out. With your other hand, carefully pull up on the plate until the pen point pokes through the plate. Now have an adult help you poke your scissors through the hole and cut around the line that you drew.

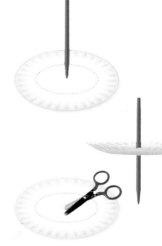

18

2 Decorate your wreath. Use markers to color your wreath any way you want.

3 Make a hook. Make a hole at the top of the wreath with the hole puncher. Thread the ribbon through the hole. Tie the ends of the ribbon together to make a loop. Now your wreath is ready to be hung up.

Other Ideas

○ Decorate your wreath with seasonal flowers or leaves, such as spring daisies or fallen leaves in fall.

○ Paint your wreath with tempera paints. Make sure the paint is completely dry before using your wreath.

○ Hang a wreath from your front door during the holidays. Decorate the wreath with hearts for Valentine's Day, shamrocks for St. Patrick's Day, eggs for Easter, stars and stripes for the Fourth of July.

Easy Yarn Art

What you need

- **One paper plate**
- **Hole puncher**
- **Yarn in different colors**
- **Scissors** (Before cutting any material, please ask an adult for help.)
- **Tape**

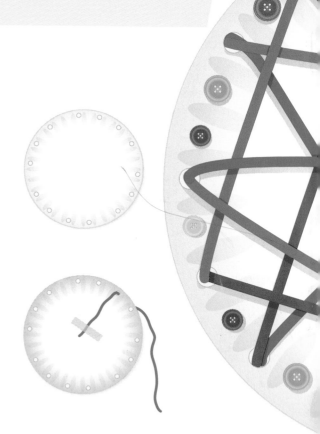

What you do

1 Make holes around the edges of the paper plate with the hole puncher.

2 Cut a long piece of yarn. Tape one end of it to the back of the paper plate. Choose one hole to start your art project. Then, thread the other end of the yarn up through that hole to the front of the paper plate, and down into another hole. Pull the yarn down through the hole to the back of the paper plate until it is tight across the front, as shown.

3 Pull the yarn across the back of the paper plate and thread it up through another hole. Then thread it back down into another hole and pull it tight.

20

4 Continue threading the yarn through the holes until you use up all the yarn. Leave enough at the end of the yarn to fasten it with tape at the back of the plate.

5 Cut another long piece of yarn, of a different color. Repeat Steps 2, 3, and 4. Repeat these steps several times, each with a different color of yarn.

6 Make a hook for your artwork. Cut a small piece of yarn and thread it through one of the holes where you want the top to be. Tie the string together to make a loop.

Other Ideas

- Use pieces of thin ribbon instead of yarn.
- Decorate the edges of your picture by gluing on buttons, pebbles, or beads.

Power Collars and Nifty Necklaces

What you need

- **One large paper plate**
- **Markers or crayons**
- **Scissors** (Before cutting any material, please ask an adult for help.)

What you do

1 Cut the ribbed edge off the plate to make a necklace or collar. Have an adult help you cut through the outside ring of the paper plate to get to the inside. Cut out the inside circle of the plate so that only the ribbed edge is left, as shown.

2 Decorate your necklace or collars. Color your necklace with markers or crayons. The possibilities are endless—make a collar like ones worn by the Viking warriors or ones that a space alien might wear or a necklace worn by an ancient Egyptian.

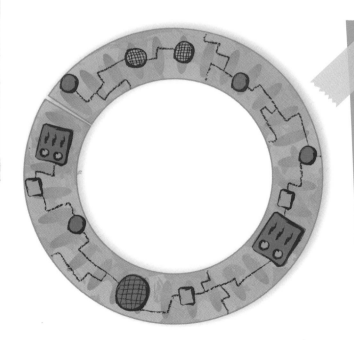

Other Ideas

○ Paint your necklace or collar with tempera paints. Make sure the paint is completely dry before wearing your necklace or collar.

○ Decorate your necklace with buttons, beads, or glitter, creating a pattern around the edge of the necklace.

Hooter the Owl

What you need

- One sturdy paper plate
- Pencil
- Scissors (Before cutting any material, please ask an adult for help.)
- Glue
- Markers

What you do

1 Make an owl shape. Using a pencil, draw two triangle shapes, one on each side of the paper plate, as shown. Have an adult help you cut out the triangle shapes. Save one of the triangles for the owl's forehead, in Step 2.

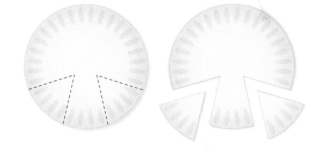

24

2 Glue the saved triangle shape to the owl's forehead. Spread a thin layer of glue along the ribbed edge of the triangle. Put the triangle on the owl's forehead, as shown. Let the glue dry before going on to Step 3.

3 Decorate your owl. Use markers to draw and color eyes, claws, and feathers on your owl.

Other Ideas

○ Make a family of owls.

○ Instead of decorating your owl with markers, use buttons for the eyes, twist ties for the claws, and felt for the feathers.

Make a Mask

What you do

1 Make the eyeholes. Using the pencil, draw two eye shapes where you want the eyeholes, as shown. Have an adult help you cut out the eye shapes.

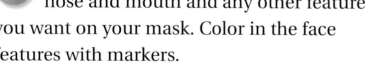

2 Make a face. Using the pencil, draw in a nose and mouth and any other features you want on your mask. Color in the face features with markers.

3. Add ears, hair, and a hat to your mask. Using the pencil, draw the items you want on construction paper. Have an adult help you cut them out. Spread a thin layer of glue to the back of each item and press it in place on your mask. Let glue dry before going on to Step 4.

4. Make a handle for your mask. Measure and mark a piece of lightweight cardboard 3 inches by 2 inches. Have an adult help you cut it out. Place the cut-out piece of cardboard on the back of your mask, near the bottom, and tape around the top and sides, leaving the bottom open, as shown.

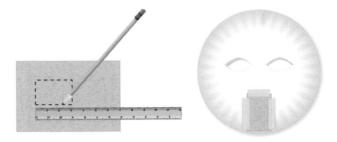

5. Insert the ruler into the holder on the back of the mask. Use the ruler as a stick to hold your mask in place in front of your face.

Other Ideas

- Make masks with animal faces. Try making an elephant, a monkey, or a cat.

- Decorate your mask with bits of yarn for the hair, buttons for eyes, or sequins for cheeks.

- Instead of making a holder, you can make a hole on each side of your mask with a hole puncher and use string or elastic to hold the mask on.

- Make a puppet using these ideas by drawing the character on the face of the plate and using the ruler as a handle to hold while moving your puppet.

Stretchy the Snake

What you need

- One thin paper plate
- Pencil
- Markers or crayons
- Scissors (Before cutting any material, please ask an adult for help.)
- Scraps of felt or construction paper
- Glue

What you do

1 Draw the snake's coils. Place a pencil point at the center of the plate. Draw a line that circles out to the very edge, as shown.

2 Decorate the coils of your snake. Draw stripes or other designs on your snake with markers or crayons.

28

3 Cut out your snake. Have an adult help you cut along the dark spiral line you drew in Step 1. Stop cutting a little way from the center of the plate to make a snake's head.

4 Decorate your snake's head. Have an adult help you cut out a tongue from felt or construction paper. Glue the tongue to the snake's mouth, as shown. Use a marker or crayons to draw in eyes.

Other Ideas

○ Make a hook for your snake. With a hole puncher, punch a hole in the snake's head. Tie a piece of string or ribbon through the hole. Now you can hang your snake up where you want it.

Stained Glass Sun Catcher

What you need

- **One sturdy paper plate**
- **Pencil**
- **Scissors** (Before cutting any material, please ask an adult for help.)
- **Bits of colored tissue paper or cellophane**
- **Glue or tape**
- **Hole puncher**
- **String**

What you do

1 Cut out shapes. Using the pencil, draw shapes on the back of the plate, as shown. Have an adult help you cut out the shapes.

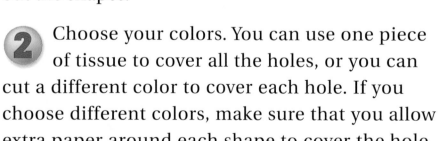
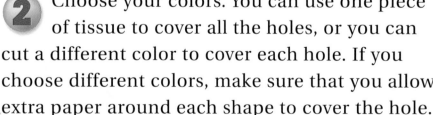

2 Choose your colors. You can use one piece of tissue to cover all the holes, or you can cut a different color to cover each hole. If you choose different colors, make sure that you allow extra paper around each shape to cover the hole.

30

3 Cover the holes. Glue or tape the tissue on the back of the plate, around the edges of one cut-out shape. Repeat for each hole.

4 Make a hook for your sun catcher. Using the hole puncher, make a hole near the edge of the paper plate where you want the top to be. Cut a piece of string 6 inches long. Thread one end of the string through the hole in

the edge of the paper plate. Tie the ends of the string together to make a loop.

Hang your sun catcher in front of a window.

Other Ideas

- Instead of making a sun catcher with geometric shapes, try making one with a happy face, a sailboat, or a teddy bear.

Index

About the Author

Christine M. Irvin lives in the Columbus, Ohio area with her husband, her three children, and her dog. She enjoys writing, reading, doing arts and crafts, and shopping.